Praise for *Roundness of the Possible*

In dazzling poetic valedictions, *Roundness of the Possible* explores cosmic evanescence and liminality. José Enrique Delmonte's poems (translated superbly by Shira Zohara Dickey) are extraordinary expressions of embodied consciousness and ecopoetics. In these poems, haunting lines such as "left-handed bees dream of right-handed futures" and "a placid whisper slows down the clocks" remind us to appreciate the beauty of transience and the sublimity of the natural world.

—CASSANDRA ATHERTON, Professor of Writing and Literature,
School of Communication and Creative Arts, Faculty
of Arts and Education, Deakin University, Australia

"Once there was the world / then there was uncertainty" writes José Enrique Delmonte in these cerebral poems translated impeccably by Shira Zohara Dickey. Here, readers are treated to the music of thinking, to poetry about thought, abstractions, essences that never shy too far from the conventional matter of poetry, the stuff of the senses. Hence, this is a very satisfying read appealing both to the philosopher and the sensualist in us.

—INDRAN AMIRTHANAYAGAM, poet, co-publisher Beltway
Editions, author of *Blue Window*

In the poem that opens this extraordinary collection of lyrics Delmonte offers a sense of his poetics. "Imminences" proposes not just an inspiritness in the things of the world but also in language, chaos and wonder; hence, throughout his work there is an ease in which image passes into image, abstraction, emotion, and thought. Cosmos, caterpillar, jasmine, "a plausible infinite closeness" and his "roundness of the possible" exist together—exist, perhaps, through each other. You can hear Nerval's sense of unity, here, as well as Lorca's mystery and Alberti's complexities.

—MICHAEL ANANIA

I had not known about the work of José Enrique Delmonte and am grateful to Shira Zohara Dickey for this accurate translation of his poetry, now made available to the readership by Marc Vincenz, Editor of MadHat Press.

—Alfred Corn, author of *The Returns*

Poet of the word, José Enrique Delmonte renews language with inspired metaphors that convey a rich and sensitive inner world. A brilliant architect by profession, Delmonte's poetry plays with spaces, urban and natural, to give an innovative significant structure to his imaginary poetic universes....

—José María Paz Gago, Writer, Full Professor of Comparative Literature, University of La Coruña, Spain

Roundness of the possible

La redondez de lo posible

ROUNDNESS OF THE POSSIBLE
LA REDONDEZ DE LO POSIBLE

José Enrique Delmonte
translated by Shira Zohara Dickey

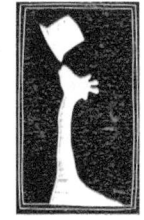

MadHat Press
Cheshire, Massachusetts

MadHat Press
MadHat Incorporated
PO Box 422, Cheshire, MA 01225

Copyright © 2017 by José Enrique Delmonte
Copyright © 2023 Translator, Shira Zohara Dickey
All rights reserved.

Copyright of the 1st edition (in Spanish, only):
Primera edición (First Edition): agosto 2017
Copyright © de los textos: José Enrique Delmonte Soñé;
© de la edición: Editorial CELYA
Apartado Postal 1.002, Toledo, Spain
Mobile: +636542794; celya@editorialcelya.com

Introduction by Jochy Herrera

The Library of Congress has assigned
this edition a Control Number of
2024937078

ISBN 978-1-952335-80-8 (paperback)

Words by José Enrique Delmonte
Cover image: *Several Circles* (1926), Vasily Kandinsky
Cover design by Marc Vincenz

www.MadHat-Press.com

First Printing
Printed in the United States of America

Table of Contents

On Time, Being, and Otherness *by Jochy Herrera*	xiii
Inminencias	2
Imminences	3
Aperturas infinitas	4
Infinite Openings	6
Habitantes del tedio	8
Inhabitants of Boredom	10
Naranjas transparentes	12
Transparent Oranges	13
En el borde	14
On the Edge	16
A veces el miedo	18
Sometimes Fear	20
Las abejas zurdas caminan con dos patas	22
Left-Handed Bees Walk with Two Legs	23
Al oltro lado	24
On the Other Side	26
Cuando el frío se desvanece	28
When the Cold Dissipates	29
Alguien dijo que somos distintos	30
Someone Said We Are Different	33
Aquel vecindario	36
That Neighborhood	38
El camino ancho	40
The Wide Path	41
Sobre equinos de madera	42
On Wooden Horses	43

Páginas dobladas	44
Folded Pages	45
El universo muere dos veces	46
The Universe Dies Twice	47
Donde mora la incertidumbre	48
Where Uncertainty Dwells	49
Ranuras en el aire	50
Slits in the Air	51
Las orugas no tienen nudos	52
Caterpillars Have No Knuckles	54
La insensatez de los vértigos	56
The Folly of Vertigo	58
Sobre libélulas	60
On Dragonflies	62
Canto de sirena para Gertrude	64
Siren Song for Getrude	66
Ingrávido	68
Weightless	70
La mirada	72
The Gaze	73
En la raíz de las cosas únicas	74
At the Root of Unique Things	76
Acknowledgments	79
About the Author	81

On Time, Being, and Otherness

Over the unfolding of civilization and since the beginning of time, investigating the meaning of our reality will continue to be a fundamental and constitutive layer of the journey of the human condition. That hunt for the self always inhabited the world of philosophy—its only and authentic problem. And in the process, that discipline revealed the nature of the truth, bringing it into the self. Of course, this unveiling of the world, gifted to us by thought, also happened in the realm of language, the arts, and particularly in poetry. Consequently, the poet, who is fully devoted to naming things and being touched by them, creates a kind of "poetic living" that includes everything essential in the world. And with that, the poet discovers the true weight of existence beyond simply reflecting on what he witnesses.

What is more, the poet must take up time as part of his or her destiny—not only as an entity that calibrates human material and spiritual continuum, but also as a frame that one lives in, grows in, and understands oneself. Better yet, as ammunition—as the pendulum of past, present, and future that represents the triumph of memory and of our individual and collective consciousness, which hopefully will make us better persons. However, convinced that perhaps their final destination was none other than death, humans became frightened by the transience of what they observed and lived throughout the course of humanity. With that, they felt anguish in the face of everything evanescent: love, nature, joy, and the *others* that inhabited their feelings.

In this book, José Enrique Delmonte (b. 1964 in the Dominican Republic), in a kind of ontological journey sketched through a solid conceptual levelness, defies the banalization of the geometric symbol. Through his words, he traces and offers a powerful representation of the totality of the circular figure: a totality in which every element of the environment inserted in non-linear time appears as an encompassing roundness of our constant and continual coming and going—in short, the course of life. In the 24 poems included in *Roundness of the Possible*, Delmonte creates a spiral of ideas from the longing, recollection, and agony of the present moment. It is a cascade of allegories that will jolt the reader until they experience vertigo. Because according to him, "Nothing escapes / From the folly of vertigo / So sublime / So light—yet it still does not escape from us."

Whether it has to do with nature, animals, or environmental concerns, the essence and imminence of things and objects, or the preeminence of the written word, as in the line, "a caravan of verbs / flees from the muteness," there is simultaneously philosophical substance and aching of the soul in this work. These are glances at a clearly wounded modernity, but a certainly possible one, in which the fear will not be the dominion of man over man, in which the birds and bees will smile while the lines that make us distinct blur. He looks at a borderless modernity, without barriers laid out on one side or the other, because, after all, we are all the same droplet occupying this chasm called life.

The vast interests that move this poet's pen are not surprising. They were previously seen in works like *Habitantes del tedio* (2015), whose verses discuss narratives about the dialogue between art, the unknown, existence, and poetic fiction. Or take the award-winning collection *Once palabras que mueven tu mundo* (2014), proof of his provocative talent as it pertains to the infinite topic of romantic love. This is no surprise, because Delmonte has a plethora of academic and professional achievements that have undoubtedly enriched his vision of existence and his creative abilities, among them the trade of architecture, the preservation of monuments, as well as a dedicated academic labor performed in prestigious institutions in the country where he was born.

In my view, the poems in *Roundness of the Possible* include hidden references to the great Neruda, such as his well-known autobiographical intimacy and deep fondness for Mother Earth; symbols of the venerated Frost, which embrace the commonplace, natural phenomena, and the everyday; and similarities with the award-winning Spanish painter and poet Juan Carlos Mestre, whose multifaceted imagery of our surroundings echoes the symbols that this poet's inquisitive pen produce.

Octavio Paz once suggested that otherness and its attendant conflicts could be successfully addressed through love and poetry. Like the loss of the integrity of the self, a symbol of the primordial rift according to Freudian thought, otherness expresses itself as a desire to find whatever is lost, or as an aspiration to confront oneself again, anxieties that decidedly cannot be separated from collectivity. The Nobel Prize winner already said it six decades ago: "So that I can be, I have to be another, find myself among the others that aren't if I don't exist." It is in this way that the poet finds every one of those others who reside in his interior, as he turns his attention to the faces of fellow human beings in his vital journey.

Generations apart, Delmonte echoes Paz when he not only informs us of the universality of the vision, "eye of much abundance … / eye of distant endings …" in "The Gaze," the penultimate poem of this gorgeous collection, but also when he gives it transcendence and permanence, as in "Infinite globe at the limit of the possible." Its function is to revolve around plurality, including flesh and the things that stopped being trapped in the flutter of the night and in any succession of latitudes. Eye-being, eye-others, imprisoned in the immensity of the present, while what we've seen shapes us, and with it, shapes memory.

Here there are profound references to otherness, when in the final text of this volume, the author buries himself at the root of things through self-imitation. He understands these things as a tactical duality, which will transcend the self to reach a double scrutinization of the other, as in the line, "I copy myself / and jealousies immediately appear / nothing about me should be so spread out / and so much more if I now share flesh / if all that I crave / multiplies and inflames / the stillness of solitude / that I now evoke." Embracing our neighbors will rescue, in the best of cases, the already quasi-lost conjugation of the verb "to be" in the present plural subjunctive: "let us be." Because sadly—and the poet confesses this in these pages—in this contemporary moment, in the 21st century, every day we are more "I"s than "others" or "us."

It is important to highlight the impeccable translation of this work in the hands of Shira Zohara Dickey, assisted by Arlene Álvarez and Rhina P. Espaillat. The result seems to have been liberated from the difficulties and obstacles intrinsic to the exchange of figures and meters between disparate languages. It is known that translation, particularly of poetry, represents an especially complex challenge, in which *what* is said versus the *way* it is said (style as opposed to content) could endanger and misconstrue the key points of the original text. In this case, Dickey's reading has resulted in the opposite. This is to say that it has led to the refinement of the metaphors and symbols that Delmonte skillfully employs.

Just like the iridescence of dragonflies' revelatory colors, which are differentiated in the presence of light and the angle of incidence, the poetic offerings of this collection discover, from the internal vision of the author, the multiple illusions and versions of reality that have interested Homo sapiens across time. Here, he reluctantly wonders if the path to dreaming has been worth it. And shaken by the fickleness of the heart, he abandons absurdity to welcome revealed feelings: "… you see the turquoise in your hand / and you know you are going back to that place / where emptiness expands / and dragonflies laugh." In such a modern, hierophantic gesture, Delmonte has invited the reader to celebrate the sacred powers of the written word and of objects, the mysteries of poetry that make the roundness of existence possible. He has done it armed with an unusual imagination and provocative symbols, in an odyssey that has given way to melancholy, fear, and the fragility of the self—without, of course, losing sight of the open promise of the future.

—Jochy Herrera
Santo Domingo
September 2022

Todas las cosas tienen su misterio,
y la poesía es el misterio que tienen todas las cosas.

  —Federico García Lorca

All things have their mystery,
and poetry is the mystery that all things have.

  —Federico García Lorca

José Enrique Delmonte

Inminencias

A Emilio Brea, a propósito

La inminencia de las cosas
toca y disloca la ficción
una hora transparente de dos caras
un silencio rebanado por la luz

La inminencia en el verbo
donde calas esas impávidas versiones
de breves apegos tiernos
de incesantes convergencias

La inminencia en el caos
la certeza en las visiones del allende
o en los quiebres del después
o en los trazos de distancias aún cercanos

La inminencia del asombro
en esos rizos que se antojan eternos
galopantes en descenso
hacia ese punto donde
se desnuda la inocencia

La inminencia en las cosas
—en sí mismo—
y al menos en la palabra
para parecer perpetuos

Imminences

to Emilio Brea, in passing

The imminence of things
touches and dislocates fiction
a transparent time of two faces
a silence sliced by light

The imminence in the verb
where you soak through dauntless versions
of brief tender affections
of ceaseless convergences

The imminence of chaos
the certainty in visions beyond
or in ruptures afterward
or in traces of distances still close by

The imminence of wonder
in those curls that long for eternity
galloping in descent
toward that point where
innocence is naked

The imminence in things
—in itself—
and at least in the word
so as to appear perpetual

José Enrique Delmonte

Aperturas infinitas

La casa huele a vestigios de gardenias
voluntades permanentes se aglomeran
un pequeño talismán de aperturas infinitas
traiciona la rigidez de sí mismo
ofrece palabras ya perdidas

En cada encuentro la casa envejece
algunos motivos la delatan:
el sofá vacío
el armario en la sombra
un mantel desmenuzado
que ya nadie admira
de las paredes brotan ruidos
colores confundidos
sellan testimonios
o conquistas

Las casa señala
el centro donde el antes volvía
al revés en las tardes
repetido en aromas
la piel ahora se cubre de albergue

Un caracol en la mano
donde comprendíamos el mundo
tantos rincones de batallas y furias
aposentada placidez en el pasado
la juventud en un instante vuelve

La casa huele a pasillos somnolientos
suena a huella de sonrisas
aun el sol la transparenta
en componenda de misterios
o de algarabías

Un pozuelo te sorprende
y caminas detrás de las gardenias…

José Enrique Delmonte

Infinite Openings

The house is fragrant with traces of gardenias
enduring desires bind together
a small talisman with infinite openings
betrays the rigidity of itself
offers words already lost

With each encounter the house grows older
some motifs give it away:
an empty sofa
an armoire in shadow
a shredded tablecloth
that no one now admires
noises spring from the walls
confused colors
seal testimonies
or conquests

The house points toward
the center to which the past returns
in reverse in the evenings
repeated in aromas
the skin seeks shelter

A garden snail in the hand
where we understood the world
so many corners of battles and rages
serene chambers in the past
youth returns in an instant

The house smells of sleepy hallways
sounds like imprints of smiles
even the sun renders it transparent
in a mysterious compromise
or in a joyous clamor

A small vessel surprises you
and you walk behind the gardenias ...

José Enrique Delmonte

Habitantes del tedio

Si cruzáramos la línea
nos crecería la barba antes de tiempo
y quedaría atrás el mito
de volar sin tener alas
o el sobre mito de parecerse al trueno
ya no sería nuestra
la magnitud del tiempo
que derrochamos apegados al fervor

Era el momento de la angustia
un paso nos borraría
como espuma en una brasa
otro nos haría grises
y nos mostraría el cosmos
de una manera confusa
era justa la amplitud
de esa ansia colectiva
que nos llenaba de peso
que nos cargaba de dudas
que nos agigantaba la pena
que nos prohibía lo absurdo

Si cruzáramos la línea
—no lo hagas—
ya no sería posible
reencontrarnos leves
seríamos barbudos siempre
e invisibles después

trasnochados y gruesos
habitantes del tedio

Tan solo una línea
y nosotros en medio…

José Enrique Delmonte

Inhabitants of Boredom

If we were to cross the line
we would grow a beard before our time
and abandon the myth
of flight without wings
or the greater myth of our likeness to thunder
we would no longer squander
such a significant length of time
in pursuit of passion

It was a moment of anguish
one step could extinguish us
like foam on an ember
another step could make us gray
and would show us the cosmos
in a confused manner
it was justified the immensity
of that collective anxiety
that was weighing us down
that burdened us with doubts
that magnified our sorrow
that forbade us the absurd

If we were to cross that line
—do not do it—
it would no longer be possible
to find ourselves frivolous again
we would be bearded forever
and later invisible

haggard, thick-headed
inhabitants of boredom

Only one line to cross
and we astride it …

Naranjas transparentes

Ahora el aire cuelga
de naranjas transparentes
te completas en la efervescencia
de sus trazos

Si partes la naranja
tu materia tu rudeza se adelgazan
entonces flotas y flotas
sobre la alfombra de tu olfato

Suceden tantas cosas invisibles
cuando alguien te permite dividirla
a un lado tan igual
a un lado tan distinto
hay caminos que estimulan
la lucidez de tus gozos

La naranja es una algarabía
de suspenso
honda… una… nueva… sola
en tus manos
asentada en tus sentidos
una naranja tiñe ahora
de utopía tu sangre

Transparent Oranges

The air now hangs
with transparent oranges
you feel complete in the effervescence
of its lines

If you split the orange
your matter and your rudeness thin out
then you float and float
on the carpet of your sense of smell

So many invisible things happen
when someone permits you to divide it
on one side so alike
so different on the other
some paths stimulate
the lucidity of your pleasures

The orange is a celebration
of suspense
sling ... one ... new ... single
in your hands
settled in your senses
an orange now turns
your blood the color of utopia

José Enrique Delmonte

En el borde

La ventaja del mundo plano
es alcanzar por fin el horizonte

Tan simple el horizonte...

Apenas una lejanía inconsistente
cargada de grafitis con el nombre
de los sonámbulos que
no retornaron nunca

La ventaja del horizonte—ahora breve—
es la prohibición del eco
por la saturación de los adioses
la delgadez de la sombra
aleja la cordura de los nuevos
habitantes secundarios

La ventaja de los sonámbulos
es que lucen despiertos para esconderse
de los sueños agobiantes
parecen pompas de jabón sagradas
suspendidas sobre su propio rito

Tan breve el horizonte...

Hay silencio en este borde
donde a veces la campana rompe
la repetición del vacío

Entonces miro atrás
y apenas veo la delgadez del retorno

Tan simple el retorno…

José Enrique Delmonte

On the Edge

The advantage of the flat world
is finally to reach the horizon

So simple the horizon …

Just a fleeting distance
filled with graffiti that names
the sleepwalkers who
never returned

The advantage of the horizon—now short—
is to prohibit echoes
by the saturation of farewells
the slimness of the shadow
removes the sanity from the new
secondary inhabitants

The advantage of the sleepwalkers
is that they seem awake enough to hide
from their overwhelming dreams
they look like sacred soap bubbles
suspended above their ritual

So short the horizon …

There is silence on this edge
where sometimes the bell breaks
the monotony of emptiness

I then look back
and scarcely see the thinness of the return

So simple the return ...

José Enrique Delmonte

A veces el miedo

A veces el miedo
mece las brasas del alfa impenitente
que conduce a la nada
vuelca la paz hacia simientes
de rugosos filamentos
se alza con las arras
de estivales desenlaces
y vuelve a dormitar
entre los vaivenes de la inercia

A veces cumbre
de espera inalcanzable
pasajero que se asoma
con versátiles mentiras
inocente instigador de retrocesos
compañero de desgarros
muchedumbre de caminos invisibles

Olor de cosas añejadas
que revela la pequeñez de la voz
borde de caídas suspendidas
en sí mismas
se asemeja al vacío
de las horas perdidas
luminaria que señala
la gravedad de las sombras

Detiene la multiplicidad
de lo posible

Roundness of the possible / La redondez de lo posible

arranca desvanece
el dominio del yo
destruye ondulaciones
en los puntos cardinales
en que una vez el hombre
fue uncido tantas veces
ahora mutante
de lo ínfimo de lo incapaz de lo continuo
suma de palabras parecidas a un arma
tanta soledad
tanta incertidumbre
tanta ambivalencia
en vuelo rasante sobre la espiga
donde descansa la firmeza
que se esfuma

A veces el miedo
es el hombre debajo del hombre
opresor de aspiraciones posibles
marcapasos en pausa
un hielo efervescente
que humedece la venganza
hasta destruir la tierra
donde cuelga nuestra voz

José Enrique Delmonte

Sometimes Fear

Sometimes fear
stirs the embers of the unrepentant alpha
that leads to nothingness
turns peace into seeds
of rough filaments
it rises with pledges
of summer outcomes
and returns to slumber
between the vagaries of inertia

Sometimes it is the summit
of endless waiting
a passenger who approaches
with versatile lies
an innocent instigator of setbacks
a presumptuous companion
a welter of invisible paths

The smell of musty things
that reveals the smallness of the voice
the edge of falls suspended
in themselves
resemble the emptiness
of lost hours
the light that reveals
the depth of shadows

Halts the multiplicity
of the possible

uproots and annuls
the mastery of the self
destroys undulations
at the cardinal points
to which man was once
yoked so many times
now shifting
with the infinite the incapable the continuous
sum of words like a weapon
so much solitude
so much uncertainty
so much ambivalence
in low flight above the masthead
where firmness rests
then disappears

Sometimes fear
is the man beneath the man
oppressor of possible aspirations
a pacemaker at rest
an effervescent ice
that humidifies vengeance
until it destroys the Earth
where our voice hangs

José Enrique Delmonte

Las abejas zurdas caminan con dos patas

Las abejas zurdas sueñan futuros en diestra
y huyen de la pesadez en las cosas inertes
duele el aguijón que traspasa mi nombre

Las abejas zurdas caminan con dos patas
cabalgan desnudas en el barro profundo
nadadoras en saliva de marsopas
rumian pasadizos de troncos
impares de mañanas tibias

Las abejas cargan la consistencia en sus alas
—diminutas alas que resaltan opacas—
las veo buscando el rojo o el ocre
en la transparencia del verde
¿ávidas de sangre?
¿rojas de melancolía?
no hay más tristeza
que la necesidad de lo ausente

Hay abejas zurdas
que derraman palabras al estambre
aquietadas en luz
celebran en silencio
cuando se abre la dimensión
de lo intemporal

Left-handed Bees Walk with Two Legs

Left-handed bees dream of right-handed futures
and fly away from the heaviness of inert things
it hurts—the stinger that penetrates my name

Left-handed bees walk with two legs
ride naked in deep mud
swimmers in porpoise saliva
they wander in passageways
on mild mornings

Bees bear consistency in their wings
—tiny wings that stand out opaque—
I see them looking for red or ochre
in the transparency of greenery
are they eager for blood?
red with melancholy?
there is no greater sadness
than the necessity of the absent thing

There are left-handed bees
that spill words on the stamen
calmed in light
they celebrate in silence
when the dimension
of the timeless opens

Al oltro lado

Al oltro lado
tan distinta la piel que se repite
no lo sé
doce campanadas pueden sonar iguales
cuando se espera nada nuevo
pero es tan distinto el rompeolas
las sendas de futuros imperfectos
los ruidos que engrandecen los aromas

Tal como me contaron
aquí la tarde se detiene
para posponer la noche
gladiolos que se abren
con una sola gota
la tierra se mueve
como si navegara lejos
lejos, lejos
un rumor de placidez atrasa relojes
se entorpecen las gaviotas en sus giros
un puñado de arcilla sirve
para afincar memoria

Este es el otro lado
tan cotidiano que acaricia las horas
un verde avasallante un azul inmenso
intensas olas
que agrandan la esperanza
he visto a las hormigas acercarse a la orilla
solo para conocer el riesgo

retornan risueñas
y se confunden entre ellas
como si fueran otras
es tan vasto este contorno
para suponernos tiernos
o tal vez concedernos infinito

En este lado
las cosas se asemejan al eco
retornan en voces
o descansan en las manos
se convierten en sirenas
o cabalgan sobre la espalda
de las hojas
basta mirar el horizonte
para saberte de este lado
no es suficiente la nostalgia
para tantas repeticiones de asombro

José Enrique Delmonte

On the Other Side

On the other side
the skin is so different that it repeats itself
I don't know
twelve bells may sound the same
when you expect nothing new
but it is so different from the breakwater
the paths of imperfect futures
the noises that magnify aromas

Just as I was told
here the afternoon pauses
to postpone the night
gladioli open
with a single drop
the ground moves
as if sailing away
far far away
a placid whisper slows down the clocks
seagulls hindered in their turns
a handful of clay serves
to settle memory

This is the other side
so quotidian that it caresses the hours
an immense blue
an overwhelming green
intense waves
that enlarge hope
I have seen ants approach the shore

Roundness of the possible / La redondez de lo posible

only to discover the risk
they return smiling
and are confounded with one another
as if they were the others
it is so vast this contour
to assume that we are tender
or to perhaps grant us infinity

On this side
things resemble an echo
and return in voices
or rest in hands
they become sirens
or they ride on the backs
of leaves
it is enough to look at the horizon
to know you are on this side
nostalgia is not enough
for so many repetitions of wonder

José Enrique Delmonte

Cuando el frío se desvanece

Al poeta Mariano Lebrón Saviñón

Una grieta se ensancha
el frío se desvanece
la caravana de verbos
huyéndole a la mudez
y la tierra—confusa—aferrada a la dureza
del tiempo que la comprime
hasta volverla un pliego
hasta destruir las voces que
sujetan la redondez de
lo posible

When the Cold Dissipates

to poet Mariano Lebrón Saviñón

A crack widens
the cold dissipates
a caravan of verbs
flees from the muteness
and the ground—confused—clings to the hardness
of time that compresses it
until it turns into a fold
until it destroys the voices that
hold the roundness
of the possible

José Enrique Delmonte

Alguien dijo que somos distintos

La tierra se divide en tantas partes
como la suma de los poros
de la muchedumbre enardecida
pueda aspirar
una línea es eso
una marca que te coloca de un lado
o de otro
y te obliga a parecerte a los quedaron
de tu lado

Hay universos que no se tocan
porque pueden convertirse en pasadizos
hacia un olvido rugoso
no sé
cuando me coloco en el borde
veo ambos lados iguales
alguien destruye la convicción que asumo
para decirme que los pendones
ondulan horizontales
que las orugas se encuentran
en la cima
y se retiran en fila hacia el pasto
donde murió la mariposa germinal

Si alguna vez dialogas en el hueco
escucharás las palabras más feroces
que aún no puedes descifrar
es la conversación entre anatemas

entre bruma de altivez
que simboliza la otredad

Incluso
hay colores que no son tuyos
que no te pertenecen
sombras que cobijan la siesta
de los que han ganado
las medallas del olvido
colores en versiones
de densidades muy profundas
que una vez flotaron a ambos lados

Hay inseguridad
cuando quieres afincar tus pasos
en la marca diluida de lo propio
se asemeja al agridulce
de las cosas intermitentes
donde pones la mirada o la lengua

Hay dolor que a veces no es el tuyo
pero los gritos de los otros te contagian
hasta prescindir de tus extremidades
te desprendes cuando sufres
te revuelcas cuando duele
te vacías cuando te llenas de tanto odio
de tantas posibilidades de infierno
sobre capas de lo que nos ha precedido

La tierra se humedece
cuando una sola gota
es capaz de aposentarse
en las grietas donde persiste la vida
a un lado florece al menos un jazmín
alimentado por las raíces
que soportan la otra parte
a un lado se humedecen las sendas
y se anegan de esperanza
a un lado
solo
la posibilidad de una mañana
o la certeza que brotará la valentía
a un lado la soledad inmensa
donde nada es tan verdad
como la mano que prohíbe el descanso

Hay tanto universos que no se pueden tocar
porque mueren al instante
como muere el jazmín que se humedece...

Someone Said We Are Different

The Earth divides into as many parts
as the sum of pores
of the inflamed crowd
that can inhale
a line that is
a mark that places you on one side
or the other
and forces you to look like the ones left
on your side

Some universes do not touch
because they can become alleys
to a rough oblivion
I don't know
when I stand on the edge
I see both sides as equal
someone destroys the conviction I assume
to tell me that banners
wave horizontally
that caterpillars meet
at the top
and retreat in a line to the grassland
where the germinal butterfly died

If you ever have a dialogue in a hole
you will hear the fiercest words
that you still cannot decipher
it is the conversation between anathemas

José Enrique Delmonte

amidst the haughtiness
that symbolizes otherness

Furthermore
some colors are not yours
they do not belong to you
shadows that shelter the siesta
of those who have won
the medals of oblivion
colors in versions
of the deepest densities
that once floated toward both sides

There is insecurity
when you want to affirm your steps
in the diluted mark of the self
it resembles the bittersweet
of intermittent things
where you direct your gaze or your tongue

Sometimes there is pain that is not yours
but the cries of others are contagious
until you lose your extremities
you let go when you suffer
you wallow when it hurts
you become empty when filled with so much hatred
toward so many possibilities of hell
over layers of what has gone on before us

The earth is wet
when only a single drop
can settle down
in the cracks where life persists
on one side at least one jasmine blooms
nourished by roots
that support the other part
on one side paths are moistened
and are flooded by hope
on one side
only
is the possibility of a tomorrow
or the certainty that courage will sprout
on one side the immense solitude
where nothing is so true
as the hand that prohibits rest

There are so many universes that cannot touch
because they die instantly
like jasmine dies when it is moistened …

José Enrique Delmonte

Aquel vecindario

> Perdonen si les digo unas locuras
> en esta dulce tarde de febrero
> y si se va mi corazón cantando
> hacia Santo Domingo, compañeros
>
> —Pablo Neruda, "Versainograma a Santo Domingo"

Las calles de piedra
las sombras crujientes
el bullicio la mugre
las ofertas el ruido
se rumian vapores
se afianzan quimeras
apuestan futuros
se gime se llora
en los días sin nombre
a mediados de abril
(como si abril fuera ahora
a mediados del año)

Las noches tan graves
con su brisa del norte
domadora de muros
con las luces (no sé)
como si fueran ostras
o puñados de niebla
como si marcharan dóciles
en la sien o en el lodo

Y los nuevos se agrupan
con sus caras de triunfo

anudados confusos aterrados
sobre andenes de sangre
de estiércol o de sal

(La calle que quiebra
las puertas abiertas
los patios que guardan
los silencios ajenos)

Tanta distancia absurda
tantas ausencias ahora
y la risa persiste
en superar aquel tiempo

José Enrique Delmonte

That Neighborhood

> *Pardon me if I tell you something crazy*
> *on this sweet February afternoon*
> *and if my heart goes away singing*
> *toward Santo Domingo, my comrades*
>
> —Pablo Neruda, "Versagram to Santo Domingo"

The streets of stone
the creaking shadows
the bustle the filth
the offers the noise
vapors wander
chimeras take hold
futures are wagered
there are city moans and cries
on nameless days
in the middle of April
 (as if April were now
in the middle of the year)

The nights so grave
with their northerly breeze
taming the walls
with lights (I don't know)
as if they were oysters
or handfuls of fog
as if marching docile
in the forehead or mud

And the new ones come together
with their faces of triumph

knotted confused terrified
on platforms of blood
of manure or salt

(The street that breaks
the doors open
the courtyards that keep
the silences of others)

Such an absurd distance
so many absences now
and laughter persists
to surpass that time

José Enrique Delmonte

El camino ancho

Ahora
el exilio descansa en el hielo
la muchedumbre del vacío
inunda el festival de la nada
la pluralidad del humo
la magia y sus versiones
ruedan en pareja leves
llueve doce veces y qué
las termitas se preservan
en rendijas de otoño
la nostalgia o la intermitencia
o la valentía de los que rumian
detrás del camino ancho

El camino ancho
tan ancho…

The Wide Path

Now
the exile rests on ice
the crowd of emptiness
floods the festival of nothingness
the plurality of smoke
magic and its versions roll in light pairs
it rains twelve times and so what
termites survive
in autumn cracks
nostalgia or intermittency
the courage of those who wander
in search of the wide path

The wide path
so wide …

José Enrique Delmonte

Sobre equinos de madera

Lo importante de esos años
no fue la tarde que obligó
a retrasar la madurez
tampoco los sobresaltos
en medio del asombro
ni las continuas lecturas
de galaxias repetidas
no fue el destino escogido
imbuidos de escozor
ni la complejidad de lo simple
que moraba en el entorno
ni la certeza de esa voz
sometida a prueba

Lo importante no fue
la grandeza de los miedos
cuando nos sabíamos
vulnerables al tiempo
ni la secuela de conquistas
sobre equinos de madera
ni la ampliación de los afectos
asentados en lazos

Lo importante...
apenas lo que queda

On Wooden Horses

The important thing about those years
was not the afternoon that
made us delay maturity
neither were the upheavals
amid astonishment
nor the continuous readings
of repeated galaxies
it was not the destiny of choice
imbued with burning sensations
nor the complexity of the simple
that dwelt in the surroundings
nor the certainty of that voice
put to the test

The important thing was not
the greatness of fears
when we knew one another
vulnerable to time
nor the sequel of conquests
on wooden horses
nor the broadening of affections
fastened with ties

The important thing …
only that which remains

José Enrique Delmonte

Páginas dobladas

Si lo hubiéramos sabido
habríamos derruido el tiempo con las manos
sin remordimientos
apretujados los segundos
que deciden la validez de las cosas
las escarchas habrían quedado
dormidas en las páginas dobladas
como cicatriz de suspicacias
como fisura de longitudes poderosas

Es tan tenue la distancia ancha
de la boca que separa la gigantez de la esencia
que allí sobresale el miedo
o se percibe la mirada de los errantes conocidos
es tan roja la esfera del pecado
que nos asumimos ruido
nos convertimos en simiente
nos trasnochamos en la nada

Y aun en la duda
confundidos con la similitud de los días
en que la bruma atraviesa la sombra
o la sombra se asemeja al alba
debimos destruir el tiempo
—si lo hubiéramos sabido—
donde la nostalgia es un hilo
suficiente para eternizar simplezas
y guardar las páginas dobladas

Folded Pages

If we had known
we would have consumed time with our hands
without remorse
squeezed the seconds
that decide the validity of things
the frost would have remained
asleep in the folded pages
as a scar of suspicion
as a fissure of powerful longitudes

It is so tenuous the wide distance
from the voice that separates vastness from the essence
that there stands out fear
or one perceives the gaze of the known wanderers
the sphere of sin is so red
that it turns into noise
we turn into seed
we stay up late in the nothingness

And even in doubt
confounded by the similarity of days
in which the mist crosses the shadow
or the shadow resembles the dawn
we must have destroyed time
—if we had known—
where nostalgia is a thread
sufficient to eternalize simplicity
and to keep the folded pages

José Enrique Delmonte

El universo muere dos veces

A Robert Frost

 La tierra en las alas de un mirlo
muere y muere el universo dos veces
las olas disminuidas en algas
huele agria
la mañana de este otoño

Dos mirlos
son la constelación posible
apretujados redondos
embadurnados de silbidos
son capaces de sostener
la sombra del eclipse
que provocan

La tierra o el universo
tal vez océanos de rayos
en el límite de la agonía
donde rumian las medusas
la memoria de sus mirlos
en este otoño rojo del retorno

The Universe Dies Twice

to Robert Frost

The earth on the wings of a blackbird dies
and the universe dies twice
waves diminishing in seaweed
it smells sour
on this autumn morning

Two blackbirds
are the possible constellation
squeezed round
smeared with the sound of whistles
capable of sustaining
the shadow of the eclipse
that they provoke

The earth or the universe
perhaps oceans of lightning
at the limit of agony
where jellyfish wander
the memory of their blackbirds
in this red autumn of return

José Enrique Delmonte

Donde mora la incertidumbre

Hubo una vez el mundo
entonces ya la incertidumbre
siempre
puede que llueva a cántaros
tal vez decidamos adherirnos al suelo
y convertirnos en sopa
puede que nos dejen entrar sin preguntarnos
a dónde van tan de prisa
si aún no conocen la lista oficial
puede que saltemos doce metros
sin acudir a las alas
inservibles en su exilio
cuando llegan los días largos
no sé si pedir las cosas
para llevar o para quedarme
es apenas un segundo
de eternidad inconclusa
parecido a la fogosidad de las nubes
puede que transite en círculos
o prefiera descender en espiral
hacia el principio de las cosas
donde mora la incertidumbre
como si fuera cierta

Where Uncertainty Dwells

Once there was the world
then there was uncertainty
at all times
it might rain like hell
perhaps we will decide to stick to the ground
and turn into soup
they may let us in without asking us
where are you going in such a hurry
if you do not yet know the official list
we might jump twelve meters
without using wings
useless in exile
when the long days come
I don't know whether to ask for things
to take or to stay
it is just a second
of endless eternity
like the fieriness of clouds
I may go in circles
or prefer to descend in a spiral
to the beginning of things
where uncertainty dwells
as if it were true

José Enrique Delmonte

Ranuras en el aire

Parecían carcajadas en descenso
o ranuras en el aire
o episodios de humedades
tanta gente que acude
a la batalla de torrentes

Nosotros asumíamos el rito
intuidos por el golpe del sureste
éramos una manada en espera
con inquietud por someternos
a su toque
la cara atenta la piel rebelde
a lo tibio a lo tenue a lo nuevo
en el estío

Parecían rumores de maracas
salpicadas de fondo
y nosotros festivos
desdibujados por las gotas
que nos vestían de halagos
y nosotros desnudos
inertes atrapados
en la inmensidad del iris
asomado a la dicha

Slits in the Air

They seemed like laughter in descent
or slits in the air
or episodes of dampness
so many people come
to the battle of torrents

We took on the rite
sensed by the southeastern wind
we were a waiting herd
restless to submit
to its touch
to the warmth to the softness to the new
the attentive face the rebellious skin
in summer

It seemed like the sounds of maracas
sprinkled in the background
and we were festive
splashed by the droplets
that dressed us in flattery
and we naked
trapped inert
in the immensity of the iris
peering into the bliss

José Enrique Delmonte

Las orugas no tienen nudos

Abrí la mano derecha
y no había nada
¡nada!
ni siquiera los nudos retorcidos
¿a dónde se marcharon?
¿quién los borró?
¿para qué podrán servir lejos de mí?
entonces pensé quizás estás muerto
totalmente muerto
como se mueren los zurdos
o se mueren los ciempiés

Si abres tu mano derecha
y no reconoces tus marcas
piénsalo
estás muerto
¡completamente muerto!
aunque escuches a los cuervos
devorar la noche
o a los arándanos
adueñarse de la luna
aunque estrieguen al oído
tu nombre
y tiembles cuando te acerques
al abismo
estás ausente
¿quién puede estar vivo
sin los nudos de su mano derecha?

Te miras al espejo
y no te ves
eso te han repetido siempre
pero es cierto
no te ves como eres
te ves como debiste ser
quizás una oruga llena de mundo
o una calamidad de residuos

En serio
todo puede ser para ti
o asumir que sigues vivo
o trasladar tus ansiedades
a otro tiempo
solo la ausencia de los nudos
te someten a la duda
sobre ti mismo

José Enrique Delmonte

Caterpillars Have No Knuckles

I opened my right hand
and there was nothing
nothing!
not even twisted knuckles
where did they go?
who erased them?
what use can they be?
then I said to myself you might be dead
totally dead
as left-handed people die
or as centipedes die

If you open your right hand
and you do not recognize your prints
think about it
you're dead
completely dead!
even if you listen to ravens
devour the night
or blackberries
take possession of the moon
even if they rub
your name
in your ear
and tremble when you approach
the abyss
you are absent
who could be alive
with no knuckles in his right hand?

Roundness of the possible / La redondez de lo posible

You look in the mirror
and do not see yourself
that is what they have always told you
but it is true
you do not look like you should
you look like you should be
maybe you are like a worldly caterpillar
or a calamity of what remains

Seriously
you can have it all
or only assume that you are alive
or transfer your anxieties
to another time
only the absence of knuckles
causes you to
doubt yourself

José Enrique Delmonte

La insensatez de los vértigos

En la espiral
los pensamientos deformados
ahora convertidos en filos
y las palabras
que una vez fueron palabras
derruidas de sí mismas

Un poco de centro
suficiente para desbordar la inocencia

Nada escapa
a la insensatez de los vértigos
aquellos ingrávidos suspensos
donde asumíamos
la longitud de las cosas
tan ajadas
que nos parecían nuevas

Tantos episodios
de estrellas conocidas
[allí Sirio
allá Celeno
tal vez Polaris]
que la espiral nos acercaba
al ojo inamovible de la noche

Aún se derrama
el olor de la melancolía
izada en episodios

donde se conjuga
la palabra viento

En la punta de los giros
colgadas en un cosmos
en láminas de firmamento
en lajas de repeticiones
similares a espejos que dialogan

Nada escapa
a la insensatez de los vértigos
tan sublime
tan leves
que aún no se escapan de nosotros

José Enrique Delmonte

The Folly of Vertigo

In the vortex
distorted thoughts
now converted
and the words
that were once words
are torn from themselves

A bit of centeredness
enough to go beyond innocence

Nothing escapes
from the folly of vertigo
those weightless suspensions
where we assumed
the longitude of things
so worn
that they seemed new to us

So many episodes
of familiar stars
[there Sirius
there Celaeno
perhaps Polaris]
that the spiral brought us closer
to the immobile eye of night

Still it is spilling
the scent of melancholy
raised in episodes

where it conjugates
the word wind

At the tip of turns
hanging in a cosmos
in sliced layers of the sky
in slabs of repetition
like mirrors engaging in dialogue

Nothing escapes
from the folly of vertigo
so sublime
so light
yet still it does not escape from us

José Enrique Delmonte

Sobre libélulas

Cuando por fin llegas a la arista
reconoces que has tocado el cosmos
¿te das cuenta que es casi un arrecife?
se parece tanto a esos bordes
entre la bondad y la incertidumbre
la tocas y sientes la peligrosa ansiedad
de dividir los antes
¡ah! emites ese grito
en medio de la nada que
se queda flotando a la espera de
algún hueco de escape
¿ha valido la pena atravesar la densidad
montado en las alas
de la única libélula sin miedo
que confió en ti?
lo sientes y te estremeces
es la primera vez que tu corazón gira
hacia el lado inverso
¿dónde ha quedado el ojo
que podía ver el color turquesa?
te convences que este es el vacío
ese instante de las cosas plegadas
sobre sí mimas
y ves las palabras que piensas
suspendidas en la punta
de la raya imaginaria del ahora
no sabes qué hacer
con tanta extravagancia posible
y te cae una gota en la cara

Roundness of the possible / La redondez de lo posible

que te humedece la memoria
y te acerca al abandono de lo absurdo
ya ves el turquesa en tu mano
y sabes que retornas al lugar
donde el vacío se expande
y las libélulas ríen

José Enrique Delmonte

On Dragonflies

When you finally get to the limit
you recognize that you have touched the cosmos
do you realize it is almost a reef?
it looks so much like those edges
between kindness and uncertainty
you touch it and feel the dangerous anxiety
of dividing what came before
ah! you emit that scream
in the middle of the nothing that
floats around waiting
for some escape route
was it worth it going through the density
mounted on the wings
of the one fearless dragonfly
who trusted you?
you feel it and you tremble
it is the first time your heart spins
sideways
where is the eye
that could see the color turquoise?
you convince yourself that this is the void
the moment of things
folding in on themselves
and you see the words that you think
suspended on the tip
of the imaginary line of now
you don't know what to do
with so much possible extravagance
and a drop falls on your face

that moistens your memory
and brings you closer to abandoning the absurd
you see the turquoise in your hand
and you know you are going back to that place
where emptiness expands
and dragonflies laugh

José Enrique Delmonte

Canto de sirena para Gertrude

A Gertrude Stein

¡Muévete, Gertrude, muévete!
navega atraviesa domina la inmensidad
de lo lejano de lo cerca
acrecienta la espera sobre las hojas
que marcan destino
¡deprisa, antes de que sea tarde la tarde!
rueda sobre cipreses
elévate hasta mirarnos
despójate de tu Olimpo
desciéndenos aposéntate en las arenas
solitarias del estío
dibújate en cigüeña
en gaviota en codorniz
y tienta la bruma donde
se adormecen las palabras
palabras que son palabras que son palabras
parecidas a tus feroces noches salvajes
a tu cobijo necesario
a tus resortes de magia
de voces y texturas
camínanos con *Yelidá*
a la orilla donde se confunden los sueños
las partidas los retornos
susurra breve a la diestra
de la *hija reintegrada*
y descubre con valentía
la historia de la *mujer que está sola*
—parecida a *Aura* a *Vicky* a *Luisa*—

Roundness of the possible / La redondez de lo posible

cuando te envuelvas en café
asómate ahora
a *la niña que quería ser sirena*
y repítele una vez más que
una rosa es una rosa es una rosa
como la vida inmensa
y tu cercanía enorme plausible infinita

José Enrique Delmonte

Siren Song for Gertrude

to Gertrude Stein

Move it, Gertrude, move it!
navigate cross dominate the immensity
of the distance from the near
augment the waiting over leaves
that mark destiny
quickly before it is too late in the day!
roll over cypresses
elevate yourself until you see us
divest yourself of Olympus
and descend for us
settle down in the solitary
sands of summer
sketch yourself as a stork
as a seagull as a quail
and tempt the mist where
the words fall asleep
words that are words that are words
like your fierce savage nights
go into your necessary harbor
to your springs of magic
of voices and textures
walk us with *Yelidá*
to the shore where dreams become confused
the departures the returns
whisper briefly to the right
of the *reinstated daughter*
and discover with courage
the story of the *woman who is alone*
—like *Vicky, Luisa,* or *Aura*—

Roundness of the possible / La redondez de lo posible

when you wrap yourself in coffee
look now
at *the girl who wanted to be a siren*
and repeat one more time
a rose is a rose is a rose
as immense as life
and your enormous plausible infinite closeness

José Enrique Delmonte

Ingrávido

Fuera de la tierra
añoro la tierra...
círculo diverso
breve de episodios y proezas
la inercia
la calamidad de las bocas
que no emergen
me persigue la faena de volver a pesar

Fuera de la tierra
y mira...
la sirena interminable rasguña la paz
el tumulto o la saciedad
el tiempo repetido en luces
la oportunidad de un hueco
o la demolición de tempestades
a mi lado un grafito y un sextante

Un vibración se asemeja al ocre
o silencio
y mira...
toco las estrellas
barbudas cicatrices
que carcomen el hastío
me molesta lo callado que no cesa
y el peligro de volver a rituales absurdos
deberías venir y dormir a mi diestra
y te contraría de la tierra
apenas una hebra convertida en puño

Ahora puedo acertar en la fragilidad
o en lo simple
supongo que sueño
un insomnio de sucesos
ahora me acorrala el polvo
o me llamas
y añoro la tierra
hueco de desgarros
donde descansa
mi voz en tu regazo

José Enrique Delmonte

Weightless

Off the Earth
I yearn for the ground
diverse circle
of brief episodes and prowess
the inertia
and the calamity of openings
that do not emerge
I am pursued by the task of returning to weightfulness

Off the Earth
and look …
the endless siren scratches at peace
the tumult or satiety
of time is repeated in lights
the opportunity of an opening
or the demolition by tempests
beside me a graphite and sextant

A vibration resembles ochre
or silence
and look …
I am touching the stars
bearded scars
that gnaw away at the boredom
I resent the quiet that does not cease
and the danger of returning to absurd rituals
you should come and sleep at my right side
and I will tell you about Earth
scarcely one strand turned into a pin

Roundness of the possible / La redondez de lo posible

Now I can get it right in the fragility
or in the simple thing
I suppose I am dreaming
an insomnia of events
now I am corralled by the dust
or you call me
and I long for the Earth
a hollow of tears
where my voice
rests in your lap

José Enrique Delmonte

La mirada

El ojo descansó fuera de sí
—sólo—en la vastedad y consistencia
ajeno a la mirada de reojo
apenas flotante en los extremos

Globo infinito en el límite de lo posible
gira se desplaza en lo plural
en lo obvio del asombro
detenida en la inmensidad
del instante
culpable de la trampa
de tantas aventuras
ojo en el espectro o
en el aleteo de la noche
repetido en sucesión de latitudes

El ojo de la carne
—contorno del orbe—
donde nadan los tiempos
sumergidos en la lumbre
errante en la orfandad de sutilezas
o en la estridencia de lo obsceno
colgado de su abismo

Ojo de tanta abundancia…
ojo de lejanos desenlaces…
perdido en la mirada de las cosas
que ya dejaron de ser cosas

The Gaze

The eye rested outside of itself
—alone—in vastness and consistency
oblivious to the sidelong gaze
barely floating at the ends

Infinite globe at the limit of the possible
rotating and moving in the plurality
in the obviousness of wonder
stopped in the immensity
of the instant
guilty of entrapment
of so many adventures
eye in the spectrum or
in the flutter of night
repeated in a succession of latitudes

The eye in the flesh
—the contour of the orb—
where time swims
submerged in fire
wanderer in an orphanage of subtleties
or in the stridency of the obscene
hung from its abyss

Eye of much abundance …
eye of distant endings …
lost in the gaze of things
that are no longer things

José Enrique Delmonte

En la raíz de las cosas únicas

Me copio
y estoy atento de mí mismo
la costumbre de entenderme doble
escudriñando al otro
en lo que me pertenece
somos dos en la misma
vibración de las cosas
me deberá caer
esa gota en mi cara
porque así está escrito
una gota es ahora
una copia de sí misma
toca la cara del que está a mi lado
entonces un millar de voladoras
se alborota
perdido en la noción de su ámbito
cuando sabe la duplicidad del tiempo

Me copio
y de inmediato aparecen los celos
nada de mí debe repartirse tanto
mucho más si comparto ahora la carne
si todo cuanto ansío
multiplica y enardece
la quietud de la soledad
que ahora evoco

Me copio
en la timidez o en el arrojo

en tantas mentiras que me calman
la agonía
en esas hazañas alimentadas
con mi lengua
leyendas repetidas con orgullo
como únicas
dueño del quizás que
se me antoja inmenso

Me copio
y comparto todo
—y digo todo—
la ambivalencia de saberme otro
en la raíz de las cosas únicas

José Enrique Delmonte

At the Root of Unique Things

I copy myself
and I am aware of myself
the habit of understanding both of me
scrutinizing the other
in what belongs to me
we are two in the same
vibrations of things
that drop on my face
must fall
for so it is written
one drop is now
a copy of itself
it touches the face of the one next to me
one thousand drops then fly
he is in a rampage
lost in the notion of its scope
when he knows time is duplicitous

I copy myself
and jealousies immediately appear
nothing about me should be so spread out
and so much more if I now share flesh
if all that I crave
multiplies and inflames
the stillness of solitude
that I now evoke

I copy myself
in timidity or boldness

Roundness of the possible / La redondez de lo posible

in so many lies that calm me down
the agony
in those feats fueled
with my tongue
legends repeated with pride
as sole
owner of the potential
that seems to me immense

I copy myself
and I share all
—and I say all—
the ambivalence of knowing myself as other
at the root of unique things

Acknowledgments

My most sincere thanks goes to the beloved Rhina P. Espaillat (Newburyport, MA), the eminent Dominican diasporic poet, author of numerous collections, and acclaimed translator. It was an honor to meet her and to receive her friendly encouragement and editorial comments. Also, I am grateful to Dr. Arlene Alvarez, a museologist, born in NYC to a Dominican diasporic family, who assisted me with Dominican vocabulary and translating idiomatic expressions. My heartfelt thanks to my dear friend, the superbly talented José Enrique Delmonte, to agreeing with my request to translate his gorgeous verses. Lastly, I thank Marc Vincenz, the acclaimed poet and publisher of MadHat Press, for taking on this worthy project.

Shira Zohara Dickey
Cambridge, MA

About the Author

José Enrique Delmonte is a Dominican architect, essayist, and poet. He has a PhD in Linguistics and Literature from Pontificia Universidad Católica Madre y Maestra. In 2009 he published his first book of poetic prose, *Alquimias de la ciudad perdida*. Since that time, he has written four more collections: *Once palabras que mueven tu mundo* (winner of the Ibero-American Poetry Prize at the Madrid Book Fair); *Habitantes del tedio* (2015); and *La redondez de lo posible* (2017), which won the XV Premio Internacional De Poesía 'Leon Felipe' in Tábara, Zamora, Spain. Delmonte has published studies about the Dominican poet Tomás Hernández Franco and the prologue to the author's book in the Classics Collection of the National Publishing House. He participated as a speaker and poetry reader at the Madrid Book Fair in 2019. In addition to *La redondez de lo posible/Roundness of the Possible*, a Spanish-English edition of *La palabra más larga/The Longest Word* will be published in 2024. The Universidad Autónoma de Honduras and the Editorial Effímera have recently published *Habitantes del tedio*, a selection of his poetry. More collections are forthcoming.

About the Translator

SHIRA ZOHARA DICKEY is a U.S.-born architectural historian, author, lecturer, and former academic society director. She also translates and writes poetry and makes fine art. Fluent in multiple languages, with reading proficiency in others, she has translated two Spanish poetry books by the renowned Santo Domingo poet, essayist and architect José Enrique Delmonte into English. Shira's forthcoming projects include publications in architectural history, a translation of another poetry collection by Delmonte, and a chapbook with her illustrations dedicated to memories of her loving companion, deceased MIT atmospheric physicist Ralph J. Markson. Shira Zohara enjoys being a Massachusetts Cantabrigian and sharing her home with two Bergers Blancs Suisses.

www.ingramcontent.com/pod-product-compliance
Lightning Source LLC
Chambersburg PA
CBHW020336170426
43200CB00006B/411